A Man's Guide To Domestic Violence

Books by David T. Pisarra, Esq.

A Man's Guide To Divorce Strategy

A Man's Guide to Child Custody

A Man's Guide to Domestic Violence

David T. Pisarra, Esq.

A Man's Guide To

Domestic Violence

LI**B**ERO MEDIA

ISBN 13: 978-0-9831635-2-7

"Anyone can be an abuser,

it takes a real man to put a

stop to it."

~ David T. Pisarra, Esq. ~

This book was written to empower men, so they may know what their legal rights and responsibilities are. So often men have no real idea of what is expected from them, and more importantly, what THEY can expect from the legal system.

CONTENTS

Section 1

What is Domestic Violence?

Domestic Violence happens when one person physically attacks another, threatens, harasses, or intentionally disturbs the peace and serenity of the other party.

Domestic Violence is painful, shameful, and damaging psychologically to everyone in the household, especially children who are frequently the innocent observers.

Domestic Violence can happen between any two people who are in a romantic or co-habitating relationship. They can be dating, living together, or married. Men and women, men and men, women and women - these are

A Man's Guide to Domestic Violence

all

The true rate of domestic violence is hard to quantify as many incidents of domestic violence go unreported. Men are chronic under-reporters of being abused, for fear of being mocked, belittled or emasculated.

There is a social perception that it is okay for a woman to hit a man, and he is supposed to accept it. That is NOT however, the law. A man has just as much right, and perhaps more of an obligation, to call the police and have them arrest the perpetrator if he is attacked by his spouse, whether it be his wife, girlfriend, husband or boyfriend.

Anyone who is experiencing Domestic Violence should obtain restraining orders immediately, men in particular should be aware of how to obtain them, and how important they are in a custody battle over children, as they can and will have a dramatic and long term effect on the rights and availability of visitation.

There are many types of Domestic Violence, it can be Verbal, Psychological, Physical or Financial. The social view of Domestic Violence has changed over the years as we have evolved from a view where women and children were the possessions of the man, to a woman being an equal under the law to a man.

Historically there were few if any limits on domestic violence, the English rule was that a man could only beat his wife and children with a stick that was no thicker than his thumb, hence the "rule of thumb." That law is no longer the case, and in its place we have gone to the rule that physically beating a wife or child is unacceptable.

Verbal

Abusing someone verbally has a wide range of meanings, on one end of the spectrum it is the mean spirited, sarcastic remark, and at the other end, it is screaming and terrorizing with threats of violence.

Verbal abuse is hard to define because so much meaning is included in our spoken words by tone and inflection. I can say "You jerk" to my partner and depending on the way I inflect the words I can convey a meaning of sarcasm, love, anger, frustration and any mix of those.

It is however safe to assume that the more curse words that are used in a sentence the greater the likelihood of abuse exists. Men frequently vent their anger and frustration using profanity. This can be seen by some people as an abusive situation. Men who yell and scream are at greater risk of being accused of verbal

4

abuse. Men who have a history of being loud and raising their voices will have a harder time explaining, if they are accused of abuse, that just because they raised their voice it was not abusive.

The law in California, and many states across the country, has become that abuse is in the eye of the abused. This makes it a very subjective matter and one that does not allow for hard and fast rules when it comes to verbal abuse.

Physical

On the other hand, physical abuse is very easily described and identified. Whenever one person makes contact physically with another, that is unwanted, it's possible to define it as physical abuse.

Physical abuse can be done with objects

also - if a glass is thrown, or a tv is tossed, or a coffee table is overturned, these are all examples of physical abuse that can result in restraining orders being issued by a court.

Psychological or Emotional

Psychological or Emotional abuse can be very difficult to demonstrate, but is perhaps the most insidious of the abuse types, because of the subtleties involved. For example, if a man tells his girlfriend that she is fat, that could be a statement of fact, but it could also be said to hurt her. A woman can call a man a pansy or a worthless coward, and that could be psychological abuse designed to make him feel badly about himself.

Emotional abuse can be the withholding of love and affection, or the intentional showering of love on another designed to hurt someone. If a woman has an affair on her husband, and deliberately flaunts it in front of him, that would be emotional abuse.

Financial

If one party hides the money and assets, that can be financial abuse. When a woman overspends or a man drinks away his paycheck, these are examples of financial abuse in a relationship. Abusing the credit cards is also a major form of financial abuse in relationships and it can have devastating effects on the marriage or partnership.

Its effects

Abusive relationships have very definite and long term effects on people. The effects are varied, depending on the type of abuse, whether it was a long standing situation, or merely a one-time drunken Saturday night. Abusive relationships usually develop over time. People do not generally find someone mean and abusive, and then fall in love. Usually people fall in love, and then the abusive behaviors develop.

Men

Generally men realize that they are in an abusive relationship only after many, many incidences of questionable behavior. Men are taught that it is their role to satisfy a woman's desires, whether they be material or emotional. So a man will persist in trying to satisfy a woman long after it is obvious that she is taking advantage of him.

It is very hard for most men to admit that they have been taken advantage of, particularly by a woman. It is even harder for a man to admit that a woman has physically assaulted him, as this strikes at the very heart of being a man. For a man to admit that a woman hit him is very emasculating. One of the first insults a boy learns is to say that someone "hits like a girl" or "throws like a girl." When boys call each other "pussies" what they mean is you're acting like a girl, a whiner, a complainer, a wimpy little boy who can't fight like the big boys.

The classic parable of How To Boil A Frog is very appropriate to how a man in an abusive relationship reacts. At first it is minor problems and disputes that are ignored, minimized or excused. As the problems become greater and the abuse becomes more regular, the man is less likely to admit that there is a problem, as he is now emotionally invested not just in her, but in how the relationship is perceived by his friends and family.

It is at this point that many men begin to experience a slow meltdown of their self-esteem and ego. As they become more abused, they also become more passive, which leads to greater abuse. The level of potential embarrassment increases with each new incident, thus making it harder for a man to admit that there is a problem.

This also leads to those situations where the abused person "blows" and the sad part is that they were essentially driven to the violence. But they will be the one going to court and jail because their behavior is unacceptable, and they didn't act earlier to prevent the damage.

Women
The dynamics of being abused will affect women as well. As the abuse continues they become more and more incapacitated, which makes it harder for them to stand up for themselves as the level of guilt and shame increases with each incident.

Children

Growing up in an abusive household creates an atmosphere of anxiety and nervousness that will have long term effects on children. The dynamics that a child witnesses between the adults in his/her life will be repeated throughout that child's lifetime. If they witness physical abuse that is not punished, it is essentially teaching a child that this type of behavior is acceptable, both as a perpetrator and as a recipient.

Conclusion

This is why fighting Domestic Violence is so important for men. To sustain their own sense of self-esteem, to stop the guilt and shame, and if there are children involved, to show them which behaviors are unacceptable and to demonstrate which behaviors are acceptable and the appropriate responses.

Taking a woman to court and asking for a protective order is not only the right way to deal with a situation that has grown out of control, it is also the best lesson a father can teach his son or daughter; how to stand up for themselves appropriately, in a civilized society.

WHO IS AN ABUSER?

Under the law, anyone can abuse anyone. There are no size limitations. There is no requirement that the abused party be unable to defend themselves. It is simply a matter of what was said or done, and how was it received.

The classic law school example of assault is that of Tiny Tim the circus star threatening to kick The Jolly Green Giant in the shins. If the Jolly Green Giant believes that Tiny is close enough, and is about to actually kick him, then an assault has happened. Assault is literally just the fear of being hit, kicked, or struck.

Now when Tiny actually kicks Jolly in the shin and makes contact, that is called a battery. It doesn't matter if Jolly suffers no pain, has no bruise, and wasn't hurt. The fact that Tiny made contact with Jolly is enough to convict him of a battery.

Under the laws of many states today, and California in particular, an abuser is someone who does an act that would be considered an assault. The laws have become very broad in what they consider to be abusive behavior. Today it begins at Disturbing the Peace of the other person and extends to murder.

Section 2

PROTECTIVE ORDERS

Temporary Orders

Most Domestic Violence cases begin with the issuance of either an Emergency Protective Order or a Temporary Restraining Order. Both of these are temporary, because they are issued against the restrained person without a hearing.

Emergency Protective Orders

These are issued in situations where a court order cannot be obtained, such as over the weekend, a holiday period, or after-hours. They are granted by a judicial officer after a police officer has asked that they be issued based on witnessing violence, or a sworn statement that violence has happened by the abused.

These are very short term orders, usually only five days, during which time the protected party is required to go to court to file for a Temporary Restraining Order in the normal course of court business.

Temporary Restraining Order

A temporary Domestic Violence Restraining Order is issued by a judicial officer, almost always based on a sworn declaration only. They are almost always granted without prior notice to the party who is to be restrained, because if they were to be given notice they would become violent.

These orders are very powerful, they can

be used to take possession of the home, the children, a business, and pets. They can prevent the restrained person from possessing guns and firearms. They can be used strategically in divorce actions to gain an advantage in finances, housing, and child custody. Women tend to use them a lot more than men for strategic purposes in divorce. Most men are not willing to play hardball in a divorce, whereas a woman will view it as "protecting her interests and those of her children" in order to justify perjury, exaggeration, and fraud.

Temporary Orders will be in force for a short period. Usually about 3 weeks, or until a court hearing can be held where the restrained party can present evidence of their side of the argument.

During that time the restrained party can be kept away from their home, their children, their business, and their finances.

Permanent Orders

Once a hearing is held on the restraining orders, any orders the court makes will be considered "Permanent Orders" and can last up to 5 years.

Permanent Orders can be renewed if the restrained person requests the court to extend the protections for additional years.

Who can get them

Domestic Violence Protection Act orders are designed to protect people who have had a romantic or cohabitating relationship. They can extend to children of the protected person and/or roommates.

What's covered in Restraining Orders?

Generally restraining orders prevent the

restrained person from contacting, stalking, harassing, communicating, threatening, assaulting, hitting, striking, or intimidating the protected parties.

This gets difficult when the parties have a child together and they have to communicate about visitation, school, medical needs etc. Frequently a restraining order will have a provision for the "reasonable communication" of the parties in regards to the children. Be careful here, because it will frequently also allow for the recording of the communications. Those communications can be used against either party in further hearings in the case.

Child Custody

Many times the sole purpose of filing a Domestic Violence Protection order is to get physical custody of the children in either a paternity or a divorce case. The court has the power to issue immediate, temporary Sole Legal Custody and/or Sole Physical Custody to the requesting party. This is a primary reason for filing for the Temporary Restraining Order. Because once that status of who has control of the children is established it is very difficult to change it.

Usually this type of restraining order is combined with a "Move-out" or "Kick-Out" order that removes one party from the home with no notice. It's a vicious way to fight a divorce or break up, but it happens frequently and if you want to win custody of your children, you have to be willing to do it.

Child Support

The court can also order Child Support based on the statements of the party who is asking the court for a restraining order. This happens less frequently, because the court prefers to have the actual information from the paying party.

Move-outs

A "Move-out" or "Kick-Out" order is one that removes a party from their home with no notice. They require that the person who is seeking to keep the house or apartment has a legal right to the dwelling. That means they must be on the deed or the lease for the court to have the right to give possession of the house to the asking party and kick the other person out of the dwelling.

These are vicious orders. They remove people from their homes with no notice, prevent them from returning, prevent them from seeing their children and pets, and can be used strategically to render the other side willing to cave in to demands quicker.

Money, Money, Money,

If there are payments that have to be made, expenses like rent, employee salaries, car payments, daycare payments, health insurance, grocery bills, these can all be court ordered to ensure that the services continue.

If there are monies to be collected, rents from apartments for example, or income from an ongoing business, the court can order one party to be the responsible party to collect the money and make sure that it is accounted for properly. This applies to married couples and couples who are Domestic Partners.

Pets

Possession and control of pets is a new category that is being incorporated into many restraining orders. For pet owners and people who love animals this a great new development, because terrorizing people by abusing their animals does occur, and this will help prevent that. Pets should not be used as leverage in a domestic dispute.

CLETS vs. Non-CLETS

"This will go down on your Permanent Record." That's what a CLETS order is. CLETS stands for California Law Enforcement Telecommunications System. If a Domestic Violence Restraining Order is entered in CLETS that means that there is a Record of it, which will show up in your background checks. This can affect your ability to get a job or a promotion, enter school, and own a handgun.

The difference is in how the orders are enforced. A CLETS order can be enforced by any police officer, sheriff, or governmental body. If a person violates a CLETS order, they can be arrested and taken into custody and then a Criminal Domestic Violence Restraining Order can be issued.

A Non-CLETS order does not get entered into a main database and will not necessarily show up on a background check. It can only be enforced by a contempt of court action, which is a civil matter.

Criminal DV

Criminal Domestic Violence is when the police have been called and there has been enough physical conflict that they make an arrest. Once someone is arrested the case is a District Attorney's case and they decide if they will prosecute it or not.

The types of crimes classified as Domestic Violence are sexual assault, rape, and battery.

Battery

Battery is the legal term for actual

physical contact between two people. It is defined as an "unwanted touching", which leaves a lot of room for interpretation.

A woman slapping a man can be a battery, a man choking another man is a battery. In the criminal courts battery is taken very seriously and is what most people who are charged with Domestic Violence must defend against.

Misdemeanor vs Felony

The difference between a Misdemeanor and a Felony is one of degree. A 'simple battery' may be classified as a misdemeanor. A more serious battery could be a felony.

You punch your buddy on the arm and it bruises – think misdemeanor. You knock out that jerk at the end of the bar who's insulting your buddy and he loses three teeth – think felony.

Felony bail

If you are arrested for Domestic Violence, in general you will be facing a felony bail situation as police officers will charge you with the highest crime that they can at the time.

Felony Bail usually begins for Domestic Violence at $50,000, which means that it will cost you an immediate $5,000 just to get out of jail – that's the bond premium that the bail bondsman will want to get you out of jail.

Criminal Attorney Fees

You will need a criminal attorney for felony Domestic Violence defense, depending on where you are, and what the facts of your case are, it will start at $10,000 and there is almost no limit to what you can spend on a criminal attorney.

Restraining Orders

Restraining Orders can be obtained in emergency situations by the police when the court system is unavailable, these are called "Emergency Protective Orders" and they are issued by a judicial officer who is "on call" and available to the police, after court hours, over weekends and on holidays.

The more common way to obtain a restraining order is to file a petition under the Domestic Violence Protection Act (DVPA). This is a form that is free to file, asking the court to restrain a person based on the declaration of the abused person. The form requires that a person sign a Declaration under PENALTY OF PERJURY stating the grounds for the issuance of an immediate restraining order. People frequently lie on these declarations in order to get immediate custody of the home, children, and pets. The first restraining order issued is called a

Temporary Restraining Order, and is issued without a court hearing actual testimony and usually the restrained person is not present.

In divorce proceedings these are frequently used to "kick out" one spouse from the home, based on allegations that domestic abuse is occurring. They can be used to require someone to turn in their handguns, stay away from a business they've built, and frequently prevent them from seeing their children.

In California once a person has been kicked out of their home based on a Temporary Restraining Order, a hearing will be set no more than 20 days later for a full hearing on the merits of the initial order. These hearings can last from 5 minutes to days. They should NOT BE IGNORED.

If someone has a Temporary Restraining Order against them, they should seek legal counsel immediately as the hearing is only a few days away and they need to defend themselves against any baseless charges.

The Reason for TROs in Custody Battles

In Child Custody battles, whether as part of a marital dissolution or paternity case, these are frequently used to "kick out" one spouse from the home, and to gain custody of the children, based on allegations that domestic abuse is occurring.

If the judicial officer, (either a judge or a commissioner) finds that a person is determined to be a Domestic Violence Abuser, which can be based on a statement as simple as "He scared me" they can lose Physical Custody of their children. The "victim" will be granted Primary Physical Custody of the children and that will affect visitation, and more importantly, it makes it extremely easy for the "victim" to move to another city or state if they want to, in order to frustrate the other parent's ability to see the children.

Why Fathers Need to Fight TROs

Once declared an abuser, the presumptions of equal parenting are destroyed. An abuser is considered to be a detriment to the health and well-being of the children and will have to go through a rehabilitation program to comply with court orders, such as anger management classes, parenting classes and in many cases a 52-week batterers prevention program.

TROs are for MEN also!

Women commit battery

Men are placed in a terribly vulnerable

position in our society, they are told they cannot hit a woman, but it is okay for a woman to hit men. Men are told it is 'unmanly' to call the police to "fight your fight" against a woman. Frequently an angry woman will call a man a coward if he attempts to call the police, and an abuser if he defends himself.

The answer is that a man MUST CALL THE POLICE if he is being abused by a woman. It is not a matter of being called a coward, a wimp, a pussy, a fag, or a loser. It is the only way he has a chance of winning. If he can prove that he was not the aggressor, which he can do if he is the one who calls the police first, then he has an argument to the judge in court. If he does nothing, he's going to lose. Any woman that is willing to hit a man, and call him a coward, a pussy, a fag, or a loser, will not think twice about committing perjury to win in court.

False Charges of Domestic Abuse

Domestic abuse and domestic violence are the same thing. False charges of domestic abuse or violence are common and in cases where there are no children, a restraining order will be issued and the couple will separate and go on their way. In families with children, the use of false claims of domestic abuse are used to gain an advantage in child custody fights.

Because a "victim" has such an advantage in court over an "abuser" in a child custody case, there is a strong motive for false charges to be put forth in court. If someone wants to gain custody of the children at all costs, they will not think twice about committing perjury.

This is why, if you have been served with a restraining order you need to hire a lawyer immediately to defend yourself.

Pitfalls of Do-It-Yourself TRO's

A temporary restraining order ("TRO") can be issued on a declaration signed under penalty of perjury, but the judicial officer who issues the initial restraining order, one that can kick a person out of their home and prevent them from seeing their children, almost never takes testimony from the alleged victim, and most of the time the "abuser" is not present or even aware that a restraining order is being asked for.

In asking for a restraining order that you have written yourself, you may not ask for enough protection, or you may put statements in your declaration that can be used against you at the hearing on the permanent restraining order. This is why you should always seek the advice of an attorney who is experienced in restraining order preparation.

A Man's Guide to Domestic Violence

Defending against a restraining order is a highly technical skill and one that requires a lawyer who knows their way around a courtroom, and the rules of evidence, and how to get to the truth of a case. Defending a restraining order that is based on lies is extremely difficult and is not something that an inexperienced person should attempt.

Defenses range from Mutual Agressor theories, Situational Conflict, Isolated Incident theories, and Defense of Others. These legal theories all require an experienced attorney to prepare and present them to the court.

Section 3

CASE STUDIES AND ESSAYS

BIG DADDY AND THE PSYCHO

Big Daddy is a bear of a man, 6'2" and 290 pounds. His ex-wife, after their marriage of 2 years, decided that even though he was good enough to sleep with, marry, father a child with, and take his money, he just wasn't good enough to be a father to their 2-year old daughter.

Mind you, he had THREE other children, by TWO other wives. BOTH of whom he vacationed with, and stayed with, and whose new spouses liked him.

A Man's Guide to Domestic Violence

Psycho, who was the one that wanted to divorce him currently, says that even though they both did drugs, and both drank too much, he was the alcoholic/drug addict and he should not be allowed near his daughter. She'd take the child support money though.

Well, that was crap, I thought, if he's good enough to be Mom's Bank, he's good enough to be his daughter's daddy.

We start playing hardball, and so does mom. She starts crying to anyone that will listen, "I think he's sexually molesting my daughter" she says. Doctors, Child Protective Services, Judges, Sheriffs, she's telling everyone that she can find that this dad is a pedophile.

She's hit the Nuclear Option Button and is not letting it go.

The courts are so concerned about this,

36

that any allegation is going to be taken seriously, at first. We have to respond loud and hard. I point out that the Doctor has not reported anything to CPS, and that CPS has closed its investigation, BOTH TIMES.

We agree (stipulate) to go through a 730 evaluation, that's where a psychologist interviews dad, mom, grandparents, teachers, the kids, anyone involved in the family, to determine who is telling the truth and who is "stretching the truth."

Throughout the 6-month process, Psycho is doing everything she can to get Big Daddy to react. He has to drive 90 minutes in Los Angeles traffic, EACH WAY to see his kid, twice a week. He does it, without complaining. And every now and then, she doesn't let him have his kid. She mysteriously "forgets" that he has visitation that week.

A Man's Guide to Domestic Violence

We call the cops on her, she tells them that she won't give up her baby, they do NOTHING. We show them the court order, THEY DO NOTHING.

She decides to move to another state, and sends Dad, AND THE JUDGE, a letter that she is taking the child with her. This is in violation of the court order. She can't do that. But we have to go to court three times to get the judge to hear the issue. Because she hasn't left the state yet, he CANNOT DO ANYTHING. She has to actually defy the order and leave with her kid, then the judge will order her back to the state, but Big Daddy will have to spend $5,000 or more, to get his kid back.

Throughout this process, Big Daddy has kept his cool. He never gets angry in an email, he's always polite, and wishing her the best. He's always good with the Psychologist, just calmly states his side of the story.

She gets crazy. She's crying in court, wailing as if she was having her heart removed through her bellybutton. She's screaming at me, screaming at the judge, the bailiffs have to escort us to the parking lot for our own safety.

Finally, the 730 is over, the psychologist says that Big Daddy needs to stay sober, and that Mom needs extensive ongoing therapy, parenting classes, and to "grow up." Also, and most importantly, THERE WAS NO EVIDENCE OF PHYSICAL, SEXUAL, OR EMOTIONAL ABUSE BY DAD, AND MOM LIES.

Dad should be allowed to continue his custody and visitation, and as the child grows be allowed to have more time with his kid.

MORAL OF THE STORY: Keep your cool, stay in the game, and let her psycho crazy crap blow her up, and you can win custody and visitation.

CHILD CUSTODY RULES FOR FATHERS

THE 3 P'S OF CUSTODY

Frequently the mother claims that the father is not a good parent, or too immature, or too uneducated on how to provide for a newborn. In this day and age I think those are weak arguments at best and disingenuous at worst. Many children are raised on formula, and while breastfeeding may be ideal, it is certainly not the only way to provide nutrition to a child.

If a man is old enough to father a child, and to be required to pay child support, then he should be old enough to take up the mantel of parenting.

Today, as it stands, fathers who want to obtain, or increase, their visitation and custody orders need to keep in mind the following:

A Man's Guide to Domestic Violence

Proximity, Paperwork, and Persistence. They can make or break your chances of getting the orders issued by the judge. Most fathers start out a custody case at a disadvantage. When dad moves out, the children are left with mom, and that becomes the way the court is inclined to keep the situation. The moment that dad moves out of the family home, is the moment that mom gains an advantage in child custody hearings.

Here's why, the courts don't want to upset the children's living environment. They focus on keeping the child stable, and that means in their historical home.

So how then does a man recover from the mistake of moving out of the house? He must show to the court that he can effectively parent the child, with as little disruption to the child's routine as possible.

PROXIMITY

This means how far or close dad lives to the child's home and school. This is a major factor in increasing, or acquiring, custody and visitation. The closer dad is to the home and school, the more easily he can be present for the child, and the courts give this great weight. If the choice is for a child to be in a car for five minutes getting from mom's home to school or a 25-minute drive from dad's home, the court is going to prefer mom's home. It is also more likely that the child's friends and social network are close to the school they attend, which is a factor for the court.

PAPERWORK

Cases are won or lost on documentation. Dads should keep a calendar or a diary of all the time that they are with their child. In any contested case, mom has something that she will use to show the court how little time dad spends with the kids.

A simple calendar which shows the days that dad took his child, and what they did on those days can make all the difference for a change in custody. If dad keeps the receipts for what he did with his child, it will allow his lawyer to prove that he took the child to see the movie <u>Cars</u> on a day when mom says he didn't visit. This is a crucial credibility issue, and one that with a little bit of work by dad, can yield big gains. The court will see that dad is truthful, and he's come a long way towards winning the credibility wars. That can lead to more time with his child.

PERSISTENCE

The biggest factor that effects whether or not a dad will win more visitation or even equal custody, is his ability to come back, time and time again. The successful dad in family court, is the dad who never gave up, and was willing to do whatever it took, no matter how difficult it was, or how long it took, to prove to the court that he wants, and is capable of being a loving, attentive, and present father.

The successful dad who wants to increase his custody and visitation, will live close to his child, keep good records, and never give up when dealt a bad hand.

WHY WOMEN PICK A FIGHT

THE RESTRAINING ORDER

The Weapon of Choice for Women

The man comes home after a long day at work, usually it's the last part of the week, when he's really exhausted. The kids are doing their homework but there's an air of discontent coming from her. He's done something wrong, but has no idea what. She starts in on him, attacking him verbally, getting him angrier and angrier. She screams at him not to yell at her, then it happens, those words, "don't hit me."

The next thing he knows. She's broken some dishes, thrown food around the kitchen, run to the bathroom with the phone, locked the door, and is calling the police.

A Man's Guide to Domestic Violence

By the time the police arrive, she's been crying in the bathroom, and prepping her story. She'll tell the police that there was a fight, he broke the dishes and tossed the food in his angry state. Maybe she'll have hurt herself to make her story more believable.

If the police investigate and find that there was some domestic violence, real or faked, the man is going to jail. Next stop – Temporary Restraining Order –ville.

Why? Because the laws have become such that whoever gets a restraining order first, has an upper hand when it comes to the custody of the children, possession of the house, and psychologically in the divorce process.

In California, Family Code Section 3044 makes it a presumption that if there was domestic violence in the family, the person who was abused, is the preferred party to have custody of the children. With that comes the control of the children's home location, and an increased amount of child support. That's what this is all about.

When a marriage is over, it boils down to money and control. If she gets a restraining order against him, the court will look at him as an abuser. Which means that he is not a good father.

The provisions of FC 3044 states that for 5 years the domestic violence restraining order can be used against the man to show how unfit he is as a parent. It will be used by her long after the 5 years are up. She'll throw it into every pleading and declaration she files in court, knowing that it will effect the court's perception of her ex. She'll use it to allow her to move out of state, to get more money from him by denying him custody of his children, and to make him feel like an abuser so that he will walk away from more of the assets of the marriage.

Men can get Temporary Restraining Orders against the women in their lives, just as easily as the women can. But generally they don't, because they live under a false impression that doing so makes them weak. Our society says that men should be strong, and "cowboy up" – which means don't cry, don't look to others for help and never appear weak.

It is a huge mistake in Family Court to live by that false credo. Men need to fight for their rights, and protect themselves in a divorce or custody proceeding. And sometimes, they need the power of the court to protect them also.

If a woman is becoming physically violent, there is no shame in the man walking away and calling the police. In fact, it is the smartest thing he can do. For himself, and for his children.

If he has been attacked, in any fashion, he needs to be aware that the groundwork is being laid for him to go to jail. He needs to stop being a nice guy, and recognize that the relationship has changed, and that he and his soon to be ex are now adversaries in a battle of perceptions. If he doesn't begin to take advantage of every tool the courts have to protect him, he can be sure that she will.

HOW TO FIGHT A LIAR IN COURT

The biggest frustration most people have in court, is the lying. In theory, no one is lying, because testimony is taken under oath. In reality, every case is riddled with lies, half truths, shades of fact and the greatest of all, the omission of a critical fact that totally changes the situation.

In the court's eyes, as a lawyer I'm supposed to be the champion for my client, and I'm expected to have vetted their testimony to make sure that it's true. Most of the time I've spent a great deal of effort to explain to the client that judges hate liars and I coach them to be as truthful as possible.

Inevitably when I get in to a child custody hearing or a divorce trial, it gets heated and the cries of "She lied!" "She's committing perjury!!" "That's a lie!" start.

In every courtroom, those phrases are said, every day. And frequently it's true. Some days it's her, and some days it's him, but no matter what, someone, somewhere is shading, spinning, omitting or outright lying.

I know it. You know it. The judge knows it.

The angry and frustrated clients always say "Put her in jail!" That's not going to happen very often, if at all. Judges can't put away everyone who lied in court, there'd be no room for the real criminals.

So what's the point of having people testify under penalty of perjury, if there's no penalty? Well, it's about credibility. Once a judge knows, or even suspects, that someone's lying to the court, their credibility goes out the window.

I had a case earlier this year, where the ex-wife testified in a Michigan court that she was married, and then submitted a declaration under penalty of perjury that she was single in a California court. The judge looked at the other lawyer and said, "so either she lied in Michigan, or she lied in California, either way, she's a liar!"

It was a bad day for that lawyer, because now they're fighting up stream with a judge who's experience with the client is that she's not to be trusted. In Family Court, when the judges are making decisions on issues like who should be the primary custodial parent, that sort of taint can kill your case.

Which is why I always advise my clients that lying is a very bad thing. No, they're not going to go jail, but they'll never have the same, and in some courts any, credibility again.

The question then becomes how to prove your case, if you know you're dealing with a liar. Fighting a lie, is like shadow boxing, for so often it comes down to this: he said, she said. Generally the best way to get rid of the shadow is to turn on all the lights and face them to your accuser and make them fight a battle that they don't want.

If my client is accused of smoking pot, we provide the prescription, then we attack with bad parenting and lack of time to devote to the child. That's how we fight a war, in which there are no winners.

"Who steals my purse steals trash; 'tis something, nothing; 'Twas mine, 'tis his, and has been slave to thousands; But he that filches from me my good name, Robs me of that which not enriches him, And makes me poor indeed.

Shakespeare, OTHELLO, Act III.

TIPS TO PREVENT SEXUAL ABUSE CHARGES

When it comes to the Nuclear Option that some Moms are using against Dad in a Custody Fight these days – CHARGING HIM WITH SEXUALLY ABUSING THE KIDS, a man needs to have prepared himself, here's my:

HOW TO BUILD A

NUCLEAR "MOM-SHELTER"

1. Have a video record of your visitations that objectively shows how you and your child interact.

One of the common complaints from fathers is that mom is misinterpreting children's "potty mouth" play. Fart jokes can be funny, but if a kid tells mom, "Dad and I were playing with our butts" it can send up the wrong red flags.

56

Having playtime on video can show how harmless your actions really were.

2. Doctors are mandated reporters, meaning if they suspect abuse, they must report it.

Be vigilant about what happened and why. When a child is taken to the doctor, be aware of HOW a question is phrased. In one case, mom was asking about a daughter's urinary tract infection this way, "Is it possible she was sexually molested?" The way in which the question is phrased makes it almost impossible for a doctor to say "No." This can be misconstrued by a nervous mother as "proof" of dad's molestation.

3. Photos are also important.

They are particularly important if a child comes homes with scrapes and bruises that mom hasn't seen before. Children hurt themselves all the time, but you should document as much as you can, so that if you need to defend yourself, you can show that the child is prone to getting hurt.

4. Keep a written diary of what you do with the kids and who was there.

Having a long list of witnesses to your parenting abilities can be crucial to cutting off allegations of negligence on your part.

5. If your ex is starting to wage the abuse war, you have to go on the alert.

Be aware of the set up situation — This is where something crucial, like a medication, has been withheld by mom and then mom calls Child Protective Services on the pretext that the child is in mortal danger. This can happen.

DON'T TOLERATE DOMESTIC ABUSE
GET A RESTRAINING ORDER

The first thing to know is that the police have a legal obligation to prevent violence. In a domestic dispute if there are sufficient grounds to believe that violence is about to occur, the police can and will issue an Emergency Protective Order. Frequently when the police are called for domestic violence, they are forced to arrest one party, whether it be the husband or wife, boyfriend or girlfriend.

If you are faced with a domestic violence situation depending on whether you are the man or the woman, you should be prepared to leave the home immediately taking with you any children.

There are shelters in every major city. Though most of them will not take a man.

59

A Man's Guide to Domestic Violence

Sexism is rife throughout the domestic violence protection community as men are vilified as the perpetrators. But don't let that stop you. More and more shelters are being built for men.

Sojourn Services for Battered Women and Their Children at (310) 264-6644 in Santa Monica. They are a clearinghouse for information and services on domestic violence prevention, and they respond to calls from women and men. When you have a dangerous spouse, the best thing to do is take care of yourself, and that means that you need to be prepared.

If the time comes in a relationship for the parties to separate, one partner frequently does not know where all the assets are located. On the flip side, the other partner frequently suffers a huge drop in standard of living because they (usually a he) will be forced out of the house at the business end of a police officer and now has to get an apartment for himself.

Most families in crisis already suffer economic hardship that now becomes devastating because they lack the financial resources to support two households. Understand that your lifestyle is going to go down, it has to, it costs more to run two households than one.

If you are faced with a pending divorce or family crisis, these are the questions you should ask yourself:

• Where are all the bank accounts? And that includes any company accounts if you run your own business.

• Where are all the stock accounts?

• Where are all the statements for the bank, credit cards, charge accounts, company accounts, pension and 401(k).

- Where are all the check registers?

- What property do we own?

Make sure you have a separate set of copies of the bank statements, credit card bills, stock portfolios, taxes for the last five years, and household bills to give your attorney. It is much easier to make copies before you have moved out.

The emotional damage a divorce causes can be extreme. You should have a good support network in place to deal with the inevitable feelings of loss, grief, anger, hurt, and sadness.

You will change friends and acquaintances, you might live somewhere different, eat in new restaurants and shop in new stores. This could be a good thing if you take this opportunity to grow and change for the better. Talk to your friends, and find a good counselor who can help with your pain.

Divorce is costly. A basic divorce is going to cost between $5,000 and $25,000 if both parties have a lawyer. If there are child or spousal support issues, or if there is property being fought over, the cost of divorce can increase dramatically.

Everyone should have a savings account before starting a divorce. Even though the money in it is community property, everyone needs quick and easy access to cash, to rent an apartment, and meet other expenses.

Be prepared for your attorney to ask for a sizable amount of money for a retainer. Some attorneys require a $10,000 retainer, others as low as $2,500, it simply depends on your case, the amount of property to fight over, and your spouse's ability to fight.

Remember that anyone can be abused; it doesn't matter if you are a man or a woman, rich or poor, white, black, gay or non-gay, Latino, Asian or Martian. It can happen to anyone, but it is not to be tolerated.

THE NUCLEAR OPTION
SEXUAL MOLESTATION CHARGES

Divorces are ugly, emotional times for most people. They get even uglier when there is a lot of property to fight over, and they are at their ugliest when a parent is using the children to extract money, and/or revenge on the other parent.

There is an alarming trend that most family law practitioners are noticing, and that is an upsurge in the allegation of child abuse by one parent against the other. Most frequently it is the mother alleging that the father is either a "bad parent" who lacks parenting skills and is only mildly abusive, to the nuclear option of sexual molestation of the children.

The definition of abuse of children has

65

changed radically over the last 30 years. It used to be common for a child to be spanked, and for some parents to use a belt or a paddle to correct their children's behavior. The book **Mommy Dearest** chronicled the path of abuse that Christina Crawford suffered from the late film star Joan Crawford, and its effects on her life, and it flung wide open the door to the topic of child abuse.

Abuse, like everything, has a spectrum, from the mildly negligent care of a preoccupied parent to the physical and mental abuse of a deranged pedophile. Our social tolerance for any type of abuse has dropped significantly, and the fighting parent who is using the children to get back at their spouse may not stop at making allegations that are false.

This type of false allegation can have serious repercussions. The father who is the subject of a sexual abuse allegation must immediately hire a lawyer who is familiar with the laws of the family court and probably also a criminal lawyer. These types of allegations are taken extremely seriously by various state agencies, and a parent who is an alleged sexual molester needs a strong defense right away. This is no time to be a "good guy" – you must fight this as if your life depends on it, because quite frankly it does.

The label of "child abuser" can destroy your life; it can take your job, your kids, your freedom, your self-respect and self-esteem and peace of mind. Your entire circle of family and friends will never look at you the same. This is not something to be taken lightly.

On the other hand, a false allegation can be prosecuted and the lying spouse punished severely by the court. The courts are taking very seriously the false allegation of child abuse and can take the children away from a parent who accuses their ex-spouse falsely. The innocent parent can, and should, be given their full legal and physical custody rights.

Mothers are the more likely parent to make the allegation that a child is being sexually molested. Frequently it is to prevent dad from getting visitation or custody, which increases the child support that he must pay. It is the nuclear option in a custody battle, and just like in the real world, it leads to the mutually assured destruction of the parties.

The emotional damage that is done to the relationship between the parents is nothing compared to the damage that is done to the parent/child relationship by a false allegation. As much as a false allegation increases the bitterness and anger between the parties, the suspicion it creates, and the spotlight of doubt that it casts on every activity causes a lasting harm to both parent/child relationships. The suspicious parent can become overly protective and begin to plant ideas in the child's mind – which is abusive in itself. The suspected parent can become tentative in offering affection and love out of a fear of misinterpretation and potential criminal penalties.

The financial damage is also extensive. A suspected parent who must hire a criminal lawyer, in addition to their family law attorney, can expect to spend at least an extra $5,000 to defend against a case of alleged sexual abuse, depending on the facts of the allegation, and there is no upper limit. I have had clients who spent $100,000 defending themselves from false allegations. And that is money that you cannot get back from the false accuser!

A Man's Guide to Domestic Violence

An allegation is easy to make, precisely because the authorities take it so seriously. The full weight of the state can be brought to bear on a father who is accused, and mothers use this to gain an advantage and make the father give in to her financial and custodial demands. And even though we say that someone is innocent until proven guilty, in this arena, even when proven innocent, there is still a cloud that hangs over a wrongly accused father. It is the fallout from the nuclear option, that never completely goes away.

ABOUT THE AUTHOR

David Pisarra has been practicing Family Law in the southern California counties of Los Angeles, Riverside, Orange, Ventura and San Diego since 1998. He has extensive experience in Domestic Violence Defense and Prosecution, Divorces, Child Support, Child Custody, Paternity, Alimony / Spousal Support, and Domestic Violence cases. He has represented men and women, straight people and gay people successfully.

Mr. Pisarra has fought increases in Alimony, and also termination of Spousal Support orders. His firm believes that testing the supported spouse for their ability to work, called vocational testing, is underused and that many paying spouses could reduce their alimony by finding out that the supported spouse could work or should at least have some responsibility to earn an income.

Mr. Pisarra has represented many fathers in paternity cases, which is a growing area as more people have children out of wedlock. Fathers have both rights and responsibilities to their children. Whether or not the child is planned, the dad has an obligation to be there for his children. It is always in the man's best interest to confirm that he is the father and if he is, to take responsibility and have an active role in the child's life.

Domestic violence protection is a painful process, but having an experienced attorney to help guide you through the mountains of paperwork, and more importantly the emotional rollercoaster ride is crucial to making sure that you are protected.